After the Loss of Your Baby
For Teen Mothers

By Connie Nykiel, RN, BSHA

Design by Janet Sieff, Centering Corporation

Original ISBN: 1-88823-100-9

Original copyright©1996

Copyright©2002
Centering Corporation
All Rights Reserved.
Revised 2004

Additional copies and other grief resources may be ordered from:

Centering Corporation
PO Box 4600
Omaha, NE 68104

Phone: 402-553-1200
online catalog: www.centering.org

*This booklet is lovingly dedicated to all my children-
John, Dominic, Joseph, Mary, Jackie, Tommy, Joni, and Becky
and their loving father Tom*

A special thanks to Sara Rich Wheeler of Grief Ltd.
for helping me to understand my grief after all these years
and for encouraging me to write this booklet.

> You are gone my dear sweet baby,
> Gone with the hopes and dreams I had for you,
> Except for two;
> That someday we'll be together again,
> and that shall be in heaven.

By Connie Nykiel mother of four miscarried babies and four surviving children

Living With Grief

Ectopic pregnancy, miscarriage, stillbirth, infant death, SIDS - these are words that have brought pain, but you may not even understand what they mean. All you know is your baby died. You may think your emotions are out of control or wonder if you have any feelings at all. Whether you lost your baby today two weeks ago, or two months ago, it is important for you to understand that someone gave you this booklet because they care about you. This booklet was written especially for teen mothers like you, to help you understand and teach you about the grief process after the loss of a baby.

MEDICAL DEFINITIONS

One of the struggles you may have is giving meaning to your baby's life. Medical definitions may not help much with this struggle, but it is the beginning of understanding.

Ectopic Pregnancy

A baby is conceived when the father's sperm is joined with the mother's egg. This usually takes place in the fallopian tube. This fertilized egg then travels down the tube to the uterus (womb) where it implants itself in the lining of the uterine walls. The embryo has plenty of room to grow here.

In an ectopic pregnancy the fertilized egg implants itself somewhere other than the uterus such as the ovary, abdomen, or the fallopian tube. Ninety percent of ectopic pregnancies occur in the Fallopian tube. There is not enough room for a baby to grow there. The tube will begin to stretch and it might rupture, causing pain, tenderness and bleeding. It is hard for a doctor to diagnose a tubal pregnancy. These babies never survive and the fallopian tube is usually removed.

Miscarriage
If a baby comes out of the womb before the twentieth week of pregnancy, it is called a miscarriage. Most miscarriages occur before the sixteenth week of pregnancy. In most cases, the fetus dies about one week before the miscarriage takes place.

Stillbirth
A baby is stillborn if it has been growing in the mother for more than twenty weeks, but dies in the uterus before it is born.

Neonatal Death
A neonatal death occurs if an infant dies before it is twenty-eight days old.

Infant Death
This is the death of a baby less than one year old.

SIDS
This stands for Sudden Infant Death Syndrome. Some people know it as crib death. It is the unexpected death of a healthy baby. No one knows what causes SIDS. It can happen any time during the first year of life.

Grief and the Grief Process

Grief
Grief is the emotion you feel after losing someone or something you were deeply attached to. This can be the loss of a baby, parent, boyfriend, home, dream, or hope.

Grief Process
The grief process is a series of phases that happen with certain feelings, actions, and thoughts after a loss. As you grieve your emotions will change often, and you will have a lot of ups and downs. These phases do not always occur in order, and sometimes you will go through more than one phase at a time. It is an ongoing experience, and just when you think you are over one aspect of grieving, a special holiday comes along and brings out these emotions all over again.

These phases, along with their feelings and symptoms, are talked about so you know what to expect. You may be surprised at how intense your grief can be, but these feelings and reactions are normal. Until a short time ago it was thought that it would take about six months to two years to work through the grieving process. Now experts think that grief is timeless and may be a lifelong process.

A Special Note

Some girls think they do not need to grieve at all because they were not attached to the baby. This may be true, and this is okay, too, but this feeling may also be part of the normal grief process and a way of denying that your baby has died. If you think you do not need to grieve, it is still recommended that you read this booklet. Hold on to it, because you may begin to experience grief a few months or even a few years from now.

The Phases of Grief

Shock

This phase usually occurs right after you have lost your baby. You may feel numb. Maybe you don't believe it yet, or maybe you're thinking, "This can't happen to me." You may burst out crying or be very angry. After expressing strong emotion, you may calm down, sleep, or just feel numb again. It is not unusual for teen mothers to feel relieved after the loss of a baby. The worry of raising a child or telling your parents may have been stressful for you. However, you still have the right to miss your baby.

Most hospitals have grief counselors or pastoral care workers who can help you through this difficult time. If the baby is big enough, they will ask you if you want to hold the baby, have a photograph of the baby, a lock of the baby's hair, or the baby's name band. If you want to hold your baby, they will allow you to hold him or her as long as you want to. Other family members should be asked if they want to see and hold the baby. Experts that work with grieving mothers have found that holding the baby brings a feeling of closeness. This will console you later on. You will be glad for the chance to have held your baby. It is scary for some young mothers to think of holding their baby. Before making this decision, know that once your baby is buried you will not have another chance to touch the baby.

If you are not sure whether you can handle looking at a picture of the baby or other keepsakes of the baby, ask someone close to you to save them until you want to see them. Being mixed up and feeling helpless are common during this time. These feelings make it hard to decide things, but this is the time when serious decisions have to be made.

You'll be asked to plan a funeral, memorial service, blessing, or naming service for your baby. Ask the baby's father, a family member, a friend, or a member of the clergy for help in making these decisions. Maybe you are feeling tired and weak and want those close to you to make decisions for you. Those who work with mothers who have lost a baby know that you will do better if you take part in making these decisions. Later you'll be glad you took part in naming your baby and planning your baby's service.

If your baby was born before twenty weeks of pregnancy, check with your hospital, a member of the clergy, or your funeral director to find out what choices you have about the final arrangements for your baby. A smaller baby or fetus also has the right to be named and have a service. You should also know that clothing and tiny coffins, as small as ten inches, are available for tiny babies.

If a few weeks or months have passed since you lost your baby and the above choices were not offered to you, there are other things you can do to remember your baby. First of all, it is never too late to name your baby or have a memorial service.

The following suggestions were given by teenage mothers who have lost their babies:
- Plant a rosebush or tree in memory of the baby.
- Have a plaque engraved with the baby's name and birthdate.
- Write a letter to your baby.
- Buy an angel in memory of your baby.
- Donate money to a good cause or a grief support group.
- Order a charm with the baby's birthdate to wear on a chain.
- Start a memory box and put in anything that belonged to the baby.

Physical Symptoms
Headaches, stomach aches, and not being able to eat or sleep are common during the shock phase. Some teenage mothers grieve by eating and sleeping more. You may spend a lot of time thinking about the baby. You may still "feel" pregnant. Your belly may still be sticking out, or your breasts may seem swollen.

A Word About Denial
The pain of losing a baby is so intense that some teenage mothers find it is easier to go on as if nothing has happened. This is called denial and is a response to grief. These young mothers can't talk about their baby. They will spend all their time working, studying, helping others, or going to parties. Sometimes they don't even attend the baby's funeral and go to school the next day. They think that if they can deny that the baby was born or was even a person, then they don't have to go through the pain and heartache of losing a baby. If you recognize these actions in yourself, be aware that for the time being it may be less painful, but sooner or later you will have to go through the grief process.

Searching and Yearning
When you come home from the hospital you may feel empty. Your arms may even ache from wanting to hold the baby. You may walk in the baby's room hoping the baby will be there and this nightmare didn't really happen. Yet funeral services or the emptiness of your home help you to realize that you really did lose your baby. You may even think you hear a baby crying when there isn't a baby there, and you may think you're going crazy. At this point you may try to make some sense out of what happened. The big question is, "Why?" This is probably a good time to ask your doctor or nurse midwife why the baby died. They may have explained this to you before, but you might have been too confused or to sad to remember. Ask for the results of any tests that were done for the baby. Be sure you understand what these results mean. How will this information affect your next pregnancy? Will there be any changes in your prenatal care?

Another feeling that will come out at this time is anger. You may be angry at your doctor for not doing enough to keep your baby alive. Perhaps you are angry at the baby's father for not being there. Close family members may anger you, especially if they caused stressful moments for you during your pregnancy. You may even blame God.

Feelings of guilt are natural but harder for younger mothers to deal with. Since teenagers are more active than adults, they worry if they danced too much or if they should have stopped taking gym sooner. Teenage mothers also feel guilty if they think they ate too much junk food or had sex too often. Even if you did everything right during your pregnancy, you still might blame yourself. Maybe you're thinking, "I shouldn't have eaten that hot sauce," or "I shouldn't have lifted my arms over my head."

Know that these are just "old wives tales" and didn't cause your baby to die. If you took drugs or drank alcohol during your pregnancy, you will be very hard on yourself. Look for a kind member of the clergy, social worker, or counselor to help you sort through these feelings. You must talk about these feelings or you might try to punish yourself in some way.

Some teen moms think they are being punished because they had thoughts about not wanting the baby. It is important for you to know that this is normal during early pregnancy. Even older mothers may be happy about being pregnant but at the same time have doubts about whether or not this is a good time to have a baby. Sometimes they wonder if they will be a good mother. This is called ambivalence. You do not need to feel guilty, because ambivalence is a natural reaction that takes place when a woman finds out she is pregnant.

Disorientation and Despair

During this time it will take all your strength just to do small tasks, such as taking a shower, getting dressed, or making a bed. Family and friends won't be as supportive. They probably have gotten over the loss and think you should be, too, but it wasn't their baby. You'll be thinking that life will never be the same. Depression sets in and suicidal thoughts are common. This may be the right time to join a grief support group or start counseling. At the very least, share your feelings with someone who is willing to listen and will not set a time limit on how long you should be grieving. If you find yourself staying home too much, try doing something that you enjoy. This can be a very dangerous time for teen mothers. Some young moms will turn to drugs and alcohol to relieve the emotional pain. This may work for a short while, but when the substance wears off they come crashing down in even deeper despair.

More drugs and alcohol will be needed to keep from feeling the pain, and drug use only delays the grieving process. Grief can never be completely avoided. By trying to run away from grief, the teenager becomes an addict and puts future healthy pregnancies at risk. If you find yourself in this situation, get help right away.

Reorganization

As time goes by you will find yourself getting through the day a little easier. You may make new friends and find new interests. You'll have more energy and feel good about yourself again. Many teenage mothers who have lost their babies think they have become more mature than other teenagers because they have learned about what is really important in life.

Acceptance

With the passing of time you will give new meaning to your baby's life, your life, and life in general. Remembering the short time that you knew your baby will bring sweet memories of a love that will last forever. Reminders of this special love for your baby will slip into every day activities and cause you to shed a few tears, but the grief will not be as intense or last as long. Some of these reminders are mentioned here so you will be prepared for them.

- Seeing a friend or relative that is pregnant.
- Baby showers or seeing a mother with a new baby.
- Mother's Day.
- Birthday parties for children.
- The anniversary of a miscarriage, due date or birth.
- Baby clothing and maternity stores.
- Hearing a child's music box.
- Children laughing and playing in the park.
- Baby magazines and commercials.
- Going down the baby food and diaper aisle in the grocery store.

Losing a baby is a major life crisis. You will always remember and love your baby, but these memories will also remind you that you have lived through a very difficult time and have become stronger. If you learn how to reach out for help, your relationships with family, friends, and God may become stronger and closer, too.

About Grandparents

Understand that the grandparents will grieve and that the grief process may also apply to them. Many grandparents try to deny their grief by telling themselves they didn't really know the baby. Grandparents also have the hard task of watching their own children, whom they love very much, suffer the loss of a child. Reading this booklet may also help your baby's grandparents.

About the Baby's Father

If the baby's father is still present in your life, and it is an ongoing relationship, then you need to know how he might react to the loss of your baby.

- Since he didn't carry the baby his grief may not be as deep as yours.
- If his grief is very strong, then he was deeply attached to the baby.
- He may be more concerned about you than about the baby.
- He may not understand your tears and outbursts.
- He may feel that he lost a part of his dreams he had for the baby.
- He may blame himself and think he did something to hurt the baby.
- He may blame you.
- He may hold his feelings in.
- He may pressure you to have another baby right away.
- He may not want help from a caregiver or a support group.
- He may turn to drugs and alcohol.

Offer this booklet to your baby's father to read. Talk over the grief process. Share your feelings instead of blaming each other. Talk to another young couple who has lost their baby, and remember everyone grieves in a different way.

Hurtful Situations

Lack of emotional support after the loss of a baby is the most frequent complaint of teen mothers. This is tragic, because teen moms are usually single parents, alone, and in need of even more support. If this is the case with you, you will need to prepare yourself for some of the unkind things that people will say and do. The discussion that follows will help you and give you some ideas for handling these hurtful situations.

Avoidance
People may avoid you or avoid talking about the baby because they feel bad and don't know what to say. Tell those close to you that you need to talk about the baby and you need them to listen to you. If a friend is avoiding you, call and tell her how much you miss her and that you need or want to be with her at this time in your life.

"You're crying too much."
People are very uncomfortable when they see someone cry because they don't know how to make the person feel better. What they don't know is that when they say "don't cry," they are trying to make themselves feel better but hurting you at the same time. Tell them it is not healthy to hold back tears.

"Get over it. It's been weeks/months now."
Many people don't know about the grief process. Everyone grieves differently and in their own time.

"You shouldn't have been pregnant anyway."
Often family members who are angry about the pregnancy will say this. This implies that you were bad and now you are being punished. This can be very hurtful to you, and can damage the relationship between you and the person who said this. You might try saying, "But I was pregnant, and my baby was a person. I miss my baby, and I need to cry for my baby."

"You were only pregnant for a little while."
It doesn't matter how long you were pregnant. Your grief can be just as deep as the grief of someone who has carried their baby longer. In some ways it may be even harder because you will never get a chance to hold your baby.

"You're young. You can have other children."
This is said to make you feel better and is not meant to hurt you. You will need to teach those around you. Say, "I know I can have other children, but no child can take the place of this child."

"It was for the best. It's God's will."
Some people think it will be easier for you to take the loss of your baby if you can see it as "God's will." This may bring out anger in you and anger at God. Remember that anger is a normal part of the grief process. However, God did not plan for your baby to die. The reality is that something went wrong during the pregnancy or in early infancy. It was a tragedy.

"At least you have one child."
If you have an older living child, or if you were expecting twins and only one lived, family and friends are usually less understanding. They expect you to be happy about your living child and forget about the one that died. This is an emotionally draining situation, because you are happy to have your living child yet you must grieve for the dead one. It is very hard to take care of living children when you are also dealing with the emotions of guilt, anger, and depression that come with grieving. You will have to let those around you know how hard it is to deal with the opposite emotions of joy and sadness at the same time.

It is said that we can only grieve as much as our family and friends allow us to grieve. Not only do you have a right to grieve, but you must grieve in order to be happy again. If you are not allowed to grieve, you may become ill and your grief may last even longer. If those around you don't know about the grief process, share this booklet with them.

Notes:

How will I know when I am ready to have another baby, or things to think over when you get that "I want a baby so bad" feeling

After losing a baby there is a strong desire to become pregnant again. For teenagers, this desire is even stronger. Teenage fathers often try to get over their grief by pressuring young mothers to have another baby right away. Below is a list of questions to ask yourself to help you decide if and when you want to become pregnant again.

Allow Plenty of Time to Grieve
- Are you hoping a baby can fill an empty place inside you?
- Do you want to become pregnant so someone will love you?
- Do you want to become pregnant so you will have someone to love that is all yours?
- Are you hoping that a new baby will help you get over the sadness that you feel?
- Do you feel alone or unloved?
- Do you have symptoms of grief such as sleeping or eating too much or too little, having little energy, using drugs or alcohol to relieve the pain, not caring what you look like or blaming yourself or others for the loss of your baby?
- Have you had other losses in your life?

In other words, have you allowed yourself enough time to grieve? Have you worked through the grief process and found answers to questions you may have had? You may have had other losses in your life, but losing your baby is probably the deepest loss you have felt. This may also be the first time you have heard about grief work. It is a good time to grieve for other losses you have had. You may be thinking, "No, no, I don't want any more grief." So here is another question for you. What happens if someone doesn't grieve, know how to grieve, or isn't allowed to grieve? Feelings become bottled up or hidden. Pain is piled on top of more pain. Some people may try to cover up the pain with drugs or alcohol. Some try to hurt themselves or live dangerously. Others use sex or run away, and some think that having a baby will take away the pain.

One teenage mother did not allow herself to grieve when her son died. She tried to lessen her pain by having another baby, but instead the grieving process was just delayed until the birth of her second baby. She had to finish grieving for her son and become a mother to her little girl at the same time. This is very difficult to do. On the one hand, grieving means letting go of but always loving the baby that died. On the other hand, you must attach or bond with the new baby who deserves 100 percent of you as a mother. You cannot do this if you are still heavily into anger, guilt, and depression. When people are grieving it is harder for them to love and begin new relationships for a while.

It takes a long time to mourn the death of someone you loved. If you have lost someone close to you, been abused or feel unloved then this feeling of loss and sadness must be worked on before you decide to have another baby. Memories of physical, verbal, and sexual abuse are also painful, because you have been hurt by someone you loved. Sexual abuse has even been called soul murder. It is known that 1/2 to 2/3 of pregnant adolescents have been raped or sexually abused. Pregnant adolescents are more likely to be physically abused. This is because they can be abused by both their parent and the baby's father. These memories need to be healed by dealing with the loss that they brought you.

It is easy to see how a young woman or man can feel unloved. It is painful to think about a parent who never makes an effort to see you or care for you. Many young people have watched a parent look for their next bottle of booze or their next hit. These parents are so addicted that they are unable to care for their children. This hurts. This is also why many teenagers want to have a baby. They want someone to love and to love them. Every day on TV talk shows young people express this wish. It isn't wrong to want to be loved, but it is unreal to expect a little baby to meet your need for love or make you feel better.

Young parents feel loss after their babies die. A new baby cannot replace another baby, replace love that you lost or never had, solve your problems, or help you feel better. If this is what you are thinking, it is a danger. When you learn that your baby needs constant care, that it cries every time it needs something, and you become tired from lack of sleep you may become angry with the baby for not making you feel loved. This is how child abuse can start. The fact is that a baby can only tell you something is wrong by crying. It doesn't mean the baby doesn't love you. It means they need someone to take care of them. A baby cannot take care of you.

When children grieve, they have temper tantrums. They get in trouble. They act up. This is because they don't know how to express their feelings. They often blame themselves for their losses. If their parents divorce, they think it's because they were bad. If they are sexually abused they think it was their fault. If a parent dies, they think it's because they wished the parent would leave them alone when they were being yelled at. Now that you are older you can grieve like an adult. That means going over all the other losses you have had and going through the phases of grief mentioned earlier.

Allow Time To Work Things Out That Upset You

- Have you taken steps to lessen the stress in your life?
- Do you get along with your parents?
- Do you get along with your boyfriend?
- If you live in an abusive family, have you taken steps to get help?
- Have problems you had before your pregnancy been resolved?

Stress may leave you with less strength to fight off disease, and infections may also cause you to go into early labor. Your baby may also be born too early if your parents or the baby's father cause you to have stress. If you live in an abusive home or are in an abusive relationship, you are more likely to have a miscarriage and 4 times more likely to give birth to a baby that doesn't weigh enough. Tiny babies are more likely to die, have physical problems such as strokes and seizures, and have problems learning in school. Teen parents have more stress than older parents. A baby born too soon may die. The healthiest babies weigh between seven and nine pounds.

Often there is less stress during pregnancy if you are married. This is because you do not have to worry about raising the baby alone. There is also money being earned to buy the things a baby needs. This may not be true if you are abused, alcohol or drugs are involved, or if there is cheating within the marriage. Whether you are single or married, take steps to change the things in your life that cause stress and worry. This is a good way to begin loving the babies you will have someday.

Allow Time For Your Body To Mature and Heal

- Are you free of sexually transmitted diseases?
- Do you follow a healthy diet?
- Do you take vitamins with folic acid in them?
- Do you avoid using street drugs and alcohol?
- Do you avoid smoking cigarettes and marijuana?
- Do you avoid parties where you can be exposed to smoke of cigarettes?
- Do you get enough rest and avoid partying all night long?
- If you are still sexually active, do you see a doctor every time you have sex with a different partner?
- Do you have only one sexual partner and has this been a long term relationship of more than one year?
- Are you sure your partner is faithful to you?
- Have you thought about postponing sex until you find a stable loving partner that is willing to make a lifetime commitment through marriage?

If you are still sexually active, you must always treat yourself as if you are pregnant. Pregnancy can take place at any time because birth control is not 100% effective. Abstinence, which means not having any sex at all, is the only way to avoid pregnancy. Many girls become pregnant while taking the pill. The effects of the pill may harm your baby. That is why mothers are told to stop taking the pill as soon as they find out they are pregnant.

Binge drinking, which means having more than 2 drinks in one night, is very bad for a baby. A baby's organs and brain are formed early in pregnancy, often before a young girl even knows she is pregnant. Alcohol abuse can cause fetal alcohol syndrome. This means the baby can be born with brain damage and/or learning problems.

Smoking affects the weight of a baby. Mothers who smoke are more likely to have a very tiny baby, and the baby can be harmed by being born too early or too small. Using street drugs can also harm your baby because your baby can be born addicted to the drug. These babies may have physical problems and later have problems learning in school.

Certain sexually transmitted diseases such as genital warts and herpes are not prevented by the use of a condom. The age of your boyfriend also matters. The older he is the more likely he is to have a sexually transmitted disease because of having sex with many partners. You are taking a big chance if you have sex with someone you have not personally gone with to a doctor to see if he is free of sexually transmitted disease. You are taking the risk of ruining not only your health but your baby's health if you become pregnant.

A healthy diet is needed. When pregnant, your body needs time to build up the nutrients needed to have a healthy baby. All women of child bearing age are urged to take folic acid. Folic acid has decreased birth defects and brain damage in babies by fifty percent.

Give your body time to mature and grow a little. Through study a lot has been learned about teenage pregnancy. It isn't good news. Babies born to teenage mothers under the age of sixteen are three times more likely to die than babies of mothers who are twenty or older. The second babies of teenage mothers are even more likely to be born too tiny, be sick or die. If your baby was born too soon, there is a fifty percent chance that this will happen again if you become pregnant again in your teen years. The healthiest babies are born two to three years apart.

Giving up street drugs, alcohol and smoking, using abstinence until you are married, following a healthy diet, and waiting until you are twenty to become pregnant again will give you the best chance of having a healthy baby.

Allow Yourself Time To Get In Good Mental Shape

- Have you tried to get over emotional pain with drugs or alcohol?
- Are you still grieving for your baby?
- Is having another baby all you can think about is ?
- Are you still angry about losing your baby?
- Are you so sad that you have little energy to get out of bed?
- If you are depressed or have been advised to seek counseling, will you take the step to ask for help?

Drugs and alcohol can numb you and take away the pain for a little while, but the pain of grief that has not been worked through will come back. Before long you will need more and more drugs and alcohol to keep yourself numb and "feeling no pain." Now you have two stresses to deal with, addiction and grief.

Anger that isn't worked through can lead to serious problems. Women who lose their babies often think of the babies as perfect angels. You must realize that if your baby had lived, you would someday have a two year old whose favorite word is "no," and the baby would not be perfect. Mothers who have babies before understanding this sometimes compare a crying baby or a busy two year old to the "perfect" image of the baby that died. Sometimes they become angry with the new baby or even an older child that they might have. They begin to wish that "the perfect child" was with them instead and may take it out on the child by hitting them.

If you decide to have another baby before you have worked through the depression that comes with grief, the depression will return after the birth of that baby. Pregnancy only stops the depression for a short time. There isn't any way to avoid the depression in grief work, not even with a pregnancy. This is because no baby can replace another baby. You will always love your baby. That love belongs to that baby and no other. You cannot take the love you have for your baby and give it to a new baby. Your new baby deserves its own love from you.

When the grief process begins again after the birth of the next baby, depression may become very severe. A young mother may not be able to take care of her new baby. Depression may drain her of energy and this can lead to child neglect. When you decide to have another baby, you must be sure it is not because you want to replace the baby or the feeling you had for that baby.

You Can & Should Love Your Baby Forever
- Have you attempted to get over your loss by trying to forget about your baby?
- Have you cut off your love for the baby you lost?
- Have you cut off the bond that you had with the baby you lost?

It is against a mother's instinct to cut off the bonds of love that she feels for her baby. You cannot love or bond to any other child unless you continue to love and bond with the child you had. This applies to children that have already been born and to any children you may have in the future. The pain of loss is so great that you may tend to want to protect yourself by never getting close to anyone again. If you do this, you will push those you love and your children away. They will see you as cold and unloving and will feel unloved. Don't listen to the advice of those who tell you to forget about it. Some people may tell you to get on with your life. You can tell them that you are getting on with your life. You are loving and grieving for your baby exactly the way you are supposed to.

Allow Yourself Time To Break Bad Habits
- If you smoke, are you willing to give it up?
- If you are an alcoholic or a drug addict, are you willing to enter a rehab program?
- If you become pregnant again, are you prepared to get prenatal care during the first trimester and lose/gain weight if you need to?

Breaking a bad habit isn't easy. It doesn't happen overnight. If you are an addict, breaking the addiction is probably one of the toughest things you will ever do. Many women say that the thought of holding a healthy happy baby gave them the courage to try. Ask your caregivers about programs that can help.

Allow Time To Finish School & Earn Some Money
- Will you be better off money wise during the next pregnancy?
- Will you be further along in preparing for a career?

Worrying about how you can finish school, who will take care of the baby, and how to pay for an education or learn a trade can cause stress before and after you have a baby. It is a lot harder to study and finish school if you have a baby to care for, and almost impossible if you have to work, too. Some young moms do finish school, but not without the help of families who are willing to babysit and provide a place to live. That's why it is best to finish school and be on the road to a career before you become pregnant.

The more education you have the better you will be able to support a baby. You will be less likely to be poor and more likely to live in a safe neighborhood. You will be able to afford doing things with your child that are fun and educational at the same time. Babies whose mothers finish college do well in school and get along better with other children.

Allow Yourself Time To Heal Spiritually

- Have you gone against your own moral values?
- Have you forgiven those that you are angry with?
- Do you feel the need to make peace with God?

Making peace with God, others and yourself is a hard step to take. We find it hard to forgive and be forgiven. Many have not been taught how to forgive or be forgiven. Finding a spiritual counselor is often the last thing we do to make ourselves feel better. Still, it is the final touch needed to feel whole again. There are so many good priests, pastors, rabbis and spiritual leaders willing to help you. They have learned to love and show compassion. They can answer some of your questions and help you find some of your answers about God and the loss of your baby. You may find comfort in prayer and strength to handle your grief. Many find new hope by returning to their church or temple.

About Your Future

Preparing to have a healthy baby takes much more than falling in love or having sex. It takes a lot of planning. Having a baby is one of the most important things that will happen in your life. It is an honor and privilege to be a mother. Remember that you are already a mother. Love your baby even though your baby is not with you. Prepare to love your next baby before it is even born. This can be done by allowing your whole self to heal, that is-your body, mind and spirit. If you have given deep thought to the previous questions and answered them honestly you will know if you are healthy and ready to have another baby.

This chapter was probably a hard one to read. It leaves you with so much to think about. It was written with honesty, so much so, that at times it probably hurt to read it. It was also written with love by someone who shares and understands your grief. It was written to give you the best chance of not having to suffer the grief of losing another baby.

Each year about 150,000 teen mothers suffer the loss of a baby. Like so many others, you have endured a terrible heartache. Some day you will realize that you are a stronger and wiser person because you have lived through grief. You will be more sensitive to the pain and loss of others, especially to other teen moms who lost their babies, because you have walked the same path. You may be inspired to start a grief support group for teenage mothers. You may want to do something for other teen mothers so they won't feel as alone as you do now.

In the beginning of this book, it was said that you were given this book because someone cared. Maybe you picked it up off the library shelf or maybe you bought it in a bookstore. In any event, know that you are not alone. There are so many wonderful people in your life ready and willing to listen to your grief and to help you become strong enough to plan a new future. Take courage and ask for this help from people that you know and admire. Try to understand those who are not able to help and support you, and surround yourself with loving and caring people who can. You will find them among nurses, doctors, social workers, teachers, spiritual leaders, grief counselors, psychologists, coaches and youth leaders. They can help and teach you to find your strengths and talents for coping with this grief. They can give you emotional support.

Honor your baby for life by getting ready to live a happier and healthier future. This is what your baby would want you to do. Take the suggestions in this book, know that they were written with love, and have faith that you will know joy again.

A Memorial Service was held in memory of:

Baby's Name:

Date of Service:

Place of Service:

Service done by:

Special Reading or Prayers:

Those in attendance:

A Letter to My Baby...

Helpful Organizations

Bereavement Services
1900 South Avenue
La Crosse, WI 54601
Phone: 1-800-362-9567 Ext. 54747
or 608-775-4747
Website: www.bereavementprograms.com

In addition to providing training for health care professionals, they offer a catalog of print, video, and gift resources such as baby rings, memory boxes, and cards.

National SHARE Office
St. Joseph Health Center
300 First Capitol Drive
St. Charles, MO 63301-2893
Phone:1-800-821-6819
Website:www.nationalshareoffice.com

National SHARE office can refer you to your local support chapter. It also provides free information packets to bereaved parents and a bimonthly newsletter for bereaved parents. Ask for their catalog.

About the Author

The author, Connie Nykiel, is a nurse journalist and teen specialist. Write to Connie at 13146 Eakin Creek Court, Huntley, IL 60142 or via e-mail at naniof4grandsons@aol.com.

For additonal copies or a free grief resource catalog contact:
Centering Corporation
PO Box 4600
Omaha, NE 68104

Phone: 402-553-1200
Fax: 402-553-0607

email: centeringcorp@aol.com
www.centering.org